BIG FIRE TRUCKS

Written by Joanne Barkan
Illustrated by Richard Walz

WHISTLESTOP®

Troll

Many thanks to Engine Company 39 and Ladder Company 16 of
the New York City Fire Department in Manhattan;
the Truro Fire Department in Truro, Massachusetts; and
the City of Hudson Fire Department in Hudson, New York.

— J.B.

Special thanks to
Thomas Osborne, First Assistant Chief,
Washington Volunteer Fire Department, Washington, Connecticut.

10 9 8 7 6 5 4 3 2 1

A Nutshell Book

The boys and girls of Miss Kane's class scrambled off the school bus. Their visit to the firehouse was about to begin. Miss Kane rang the doorbell. A few seconds later a woman wearing a blue shirt and pants opened the door.

"Welcome to the firehouse," the woman said. "I'm Pam—one of the firefighters. Come on in!"

Pam led the children to the fire trucks.

"The two most important kinds of fire trucks are ladders and engines," she said. "Another name for *engine* is *pumper.* Let's take a look at one."

Pam explained that every engine has a powerful pump that sucks water through a hose from a fire hydrant to the truck. Then the pump forces the water through other hoses, which the firefighters use to put out the fire.

"The engine also carries lots of equipment," Pam added. "There are fire extinguishers, bolt cutters, ropes, blankets, a first-aid kit, and almost half a mile of folded-up hose!"

"Now let's look at the ladder truck," Pam said. "The big ladder can reach the top of a seven-story building. It's mounted on a turntable, so we can turn the ladder in any direction."

Pam pointed out the stabilizer legs that hold the truck steady when the ladder is raised. She showed everyone the truck's other equipment, including portable ladders, axes, and hooks.

"Firefighters must rescue people trapped in burning buildings," she explained. "Sometimes we need to use axes and hooks to break through doors, walls, and floors."

A firefighter named Harry took the children upstairs to see the rest of the firehouse.

"This is the locker room," he said. "We keep our street clothes in the lockers. There are showers here, too, so we can wash up after work."

Harry showed the children the office where the firefighters did their paperwork, the bunk room they rested in, and the kitchen.

"We all take turns shopping for food and cooking," Harry explained. "The day shift eats lunch here, and the night shift eats dinner."

Harry led the children downstairs.
"We have plenty of work to do between fires," he said.
"We clean and repair the equipment, and we have drills
to practice fire fighting."

Harry pointed to a metal pole that ran from the first floor all the way up to the ceiling of the second floor.

"Who knows what this is for?" he asked, pointing to the pole.

But before anyone could say a word, a loud noise rang through the firehouse. *BRRRINNNGG! BRRRINNNGG! BRRRINNNGG! BRRRINNNGG! BRRRINNNGG!*

WHOOSH! WHOOSH! WHOOSH! Three firefighters slid down the metal pole from the second floor to the first.

All the firefighters ran toward the trucks. Their tall rubber boots were standing close by. A pair of thickly padded pants was carefully arranged around each pair of boots. The firefighters kicked off their shoes, jumped into their boots, and yanked up the heavy pants.

The firefighters quickly pulled on the rest of their gear: helmets, coats, and leather gloves. Harry, Pam, and several other firefighters leaped into the pumper. Harry got behind the steering wheel.

The children stayed safely out of the way and watched as the big firehouse doors opened. With sirens wailing, horns blowing, and red lights flashing, the trucks sped out of the firehouse.

From the other part of town the fire chief rushed to the fire in his four-wheel-drive truck. It was bright red and had the fire department's insignia painted on its sides. A bar of red lights flashed on the roof. The truck's siren blared.

The fire chief commanded all six firehouses in the district. He had a two-way radio and a car phone inside his truck. "Chief to dispatcher," he said into the radio transmitter. "First alarm. Structure fire. Warehouse on Collins Street."

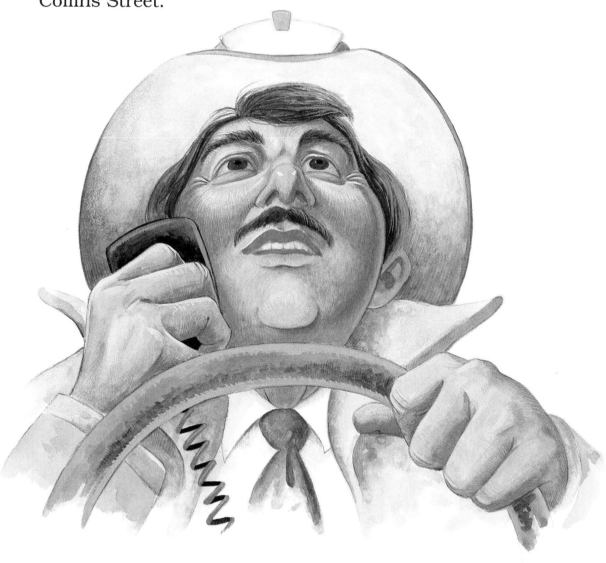

The fire chief's truck screeched to a stop in front of the blazing warehouse. The chief jumped out and looked at the scene.

Harry and Pam were already aiming a stream of water at the fire. They had hooked up their hose directly to the 500-gallon water tank in the pumper. Some firefighters connected hoses to a fire hydrant. Others carried hoses toward the warehouse. Still others raised the ladder and broke open windows and doors with axes. They had to let the smoke and heat out of the building.

One firefighter stopped traffic, including the school bus carrying Miss Kane and her class. "Please wait here," the firefighter said to the school bus driver. "We've closed the surrounding streets for a while."

"Well, it looks like we're going to see our fire department in action!" Miss Kane said.

"This blaze could spread to the sports center next door!" the chief told one of the firefighters. He grabbed his radio. "I'm calling in a second alarm." This meant he was calling for a second group of fire trucks.

Three minutes later an engine and a tower ladder truck arrived from another firehouse. Two firefighters jumped into the bucket at the end of the truck's folded ladder. The ladder rose into the air, carrying the firefighters close to the warehouse roof. The second engine pumped water into the tower ladder truck. The water rushed through a pipe that ran up to the top of the ladder. *WHOOSH!* The firefighters in the bucket aimed the water nozzle at the burning roof.

Just then a rescue truck and an ambulance arrived
with their lights flashing.
  "There's a man still in the building," the fire chief said.
"Let's get him out safely."

The firefighters pulled open the rescue truck's storage compartments. Inside were many types of rescue equipment: sledgehammers, tow chains, power saws, hydraulic jacks, inflatable rafts, and even scuba-diving gear. They took out a steel-cutting tool called the "jaws of life" and raced toward the smoke-filled building. They put on face masks and air tanks as they ran.

Two emergency medical technicians leaped out of the ambulance and opened the back doors. Inside were cabinets filled with medical supplies, a long bench, a desk, a telephone, and a stretcher.

Firefighters pulled the stretcher out of the ambulance and ran with it toward the warehouse. But just as they got there, a man walked out of the building helped by two firefighters.

"This man is the warehouse guard," one of the firefighters said to the chief. "He inhaled some smoke, but other than that, he's okay."

A team of firefighters searched the warehouse for other trapped people, but they didn't find anyone else. Other firefighters cut a large hole in the roof to get to the fire more easily. They used every hose to soak the building, inside and out. They finally got the blaze under control. Before long the fire was out.

A firefighter opened the street to traffic. As the school bus drove past the warehouse, the children in Miss Kane's class waved to the firefighters and shouted, "Good- bye!"

The fire chief went inside to inspect the warehouse. "Good work!" he said to the firefighters. "You saved the guard's life and kept this fire from spreading. You did a fine job!"

The tired firefighters packed up all their equipment. Pam and Harry checked the hoses for damage, and then rolled them up neatly and restacked them in the engine.

Back in the firehouse the firefighters cleaned and checked the rest of the equipment. They refilled the engine's water tank and fuel tank. The firehouse had its own diesel fuel pump.

The firefighters washed up quickly. They were
ready to fight another fire if the alarm rang. While
they waited, some rested in the bunk room, and
others watched television. Several ate snacks.

Harry was arranging his boots and pants when he noticed something lying on the floor.

"Look what I found," he said, holding up a small jacket. "This must belong to one of the school children who visited us today."

The next morning Harry stopped by Miss Kane's classroom to return the jacket. He waved to the children and said, "We hope to see you at the firehouse again soon."